visual
magic

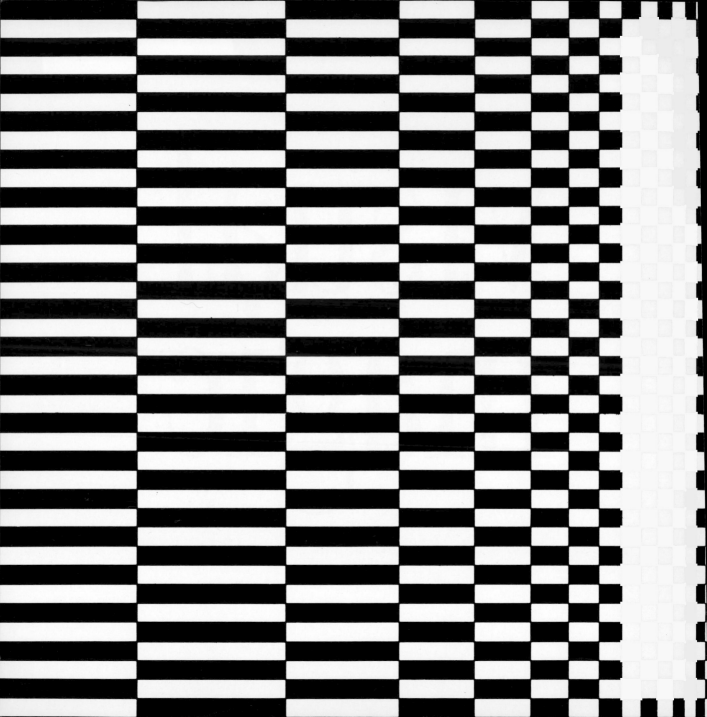

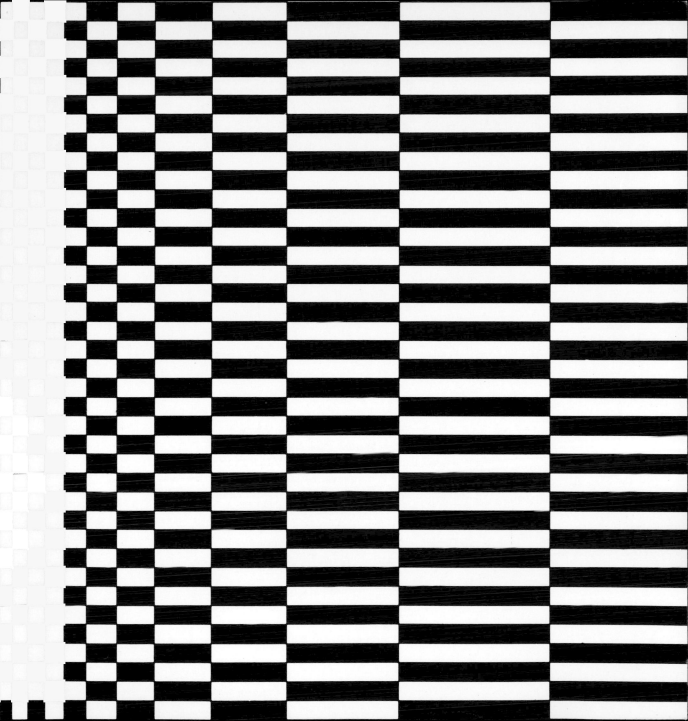

2 4 6 8 10 9 7 5 3

First paperback edition published
in 2000 by Sterling Publishing Company, Inc.
387 Park Avenue South, New York, N.Y. 10016
Originally published in hardcover by Dial Books for Young Readers
Conceived and produced by Breslich & Foss Limited, London
© 1991 by Breslich & Foss Limited
Distributed in Canada by Sterling Publishing
c/o Canadian Manda Group, One Atlantic Avenue, Suite 105
Toronto, Ontario, Canada M6K 3E7

Printed in China

Sterling ISBN 0-8069-5815-4

Dr. David Thomson

visual magic

Sterling Publishing Co., Inc.
New York

Acknowledgments

Leonardo da Vinci ''Mona Lisa'' on page 56, by courtesy of the Louvre, Paris/Bridgeman Art Library

Giuseppe Arcimboldo ''The Vegetable Gardener'' on page 27, by courtesy of Museo Civico Ala Ponzone, Cremona/Bridgeman Art Library. ''Water'' on page 31, by courtesy of Kunsthistorischen Museum, Vienna.

Illustration on page 5 © Weidenfeld & Nicholson Ltd. (Ronald C. James); page 18 © Keith Kay; pages 15, 21, 25 © David Thomson; page 35 © Jean Larcher/Dover Books; page 37 © The Art and Science of Visual Illusions by Nicholas Wade, Routledge; page 40 © Lawrence Whistler; page 56 © Mander & Mitchenson

Illustrations on pages 16, 17, 39 by Aziz Khan
Illustrations on pages 7, 11, 19, 42, 43, 47, 51, 55 by Ivan Ripley
Photograph on page 29 by Brooke Calverley
Illustration on page 33 by Guy Davies

Introduction

Is there a hidden face in this picture? Are these lines straight or curved? Is this shape moving? If so, which way?

These are just a few of the fun questions that are asked in the pages of *Visual Magic*. Included are over thirty tricks and illusions that will keep you fascinated and delighted, as something you are sure you see changes before your eyes.

How is this possible? The eyes are like miniature cameras. They take images of what we see and send information about these images to the brain to decide what this information means. Together the eyes and brain make up our visual system, which is usually very good at making sense of the world around us. But sometimes it is possible to *trick* our visual system. Lines can look longer or shorter than they really are, a random pattern of squares can suddenly become a face, or—with special glasses found at the back of the book—a dotted pattern will come toward you in 3-D splendor. These are all visual illusions.

What follows is a wide range of visual illusions. Some take just a few seconds, others take longer. Most can be done alone, but some are easier with a friend. Different people will find different illusions trickier. A few of the more commonly difficult tricks have clues provided or an answer given in the key at the back of the book. All of the visual tricks offer wonderful insights into how our visual systems are altered by a variety of factors.

So turn the page and enjoy the visual magic that unfolds!

Spot the Dog

This "picture" looks like a series of black spots on a white page, with no particular shape. There is a picture hidden within the spots, but your eyes and brain need to work to discover it. Once you have found the secret picture, close the book for a moment and then look again — how long does it take to see it this time?

The Vanishing Goldfish

Hold the book near your face and close your left eye. Stare at the cat's nose with your right eye and then move the book slowly away from you. Suddenly the goldfish will vanish.

The goldfish disappears within your eye's "blind spot." The picture has been carefully arranged so that when the image is a certain distance away, you are looking at the goldfish with a small part of the eye that cannot see. This part is called the "optic disk."

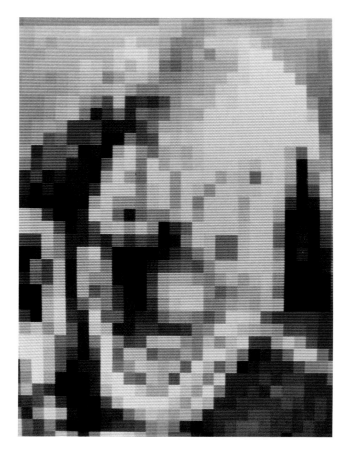

Who Am I?

Study the picture on the left. Can you see what it is? Hold the book at arm's length. . . . A picture should begin to emerge from the mass of squares. Prop up the book and look at the picture, slowly backing away from it. The further away you get, the clearer the picture will become. (Sometimes it helps to "squint" your eyes slightly.)

This picture was produced by feeding an ordinary photograph into a computer. The computer divided it into a series of squares.

This has also been done to a picture of a very famous face (see opposite). Who is it? Turn to page 56 for the answers.

<u>Toward the Vanishing Point</u>

Here are two goats, Duane and Clarence. Which do you think is bigger? Measure them to find out whether your guess is correct.

Duane and Clarence are actually the same size, but Clarence looks larger because he appears to be further away than Duane. Normally as an object gets further away, the real image gets smaller, but our brains work out the actual size by a clever calculation that compares the size of the image with an estimate of how far away the object is. In this picture it is the vanishing lines that trick our brain into thinking Clarence is further away than Duane.

The After Image

Take a piece of plain white paper, and place it beside the book. Hold the book under a bright light and stare at the black dot in the middle of the image opposite for about thirty seconds, trying not to blink. Now look at the white paper and keep blinking your eyes. Who has appeared?

The image actually printed here is called a negative image—white is printed as black and black as white. When you stare at the white paper after staring at the negative image for a while, your eye reverses the image and sees a positive one. This reversed picture is called an "after image."

If you now look at a light-colored wall from a distance (such as, across the room) and continue to blink, the same after image, only larger, will appear. To discover the identity of this person, turn to page 56.

Strange Fruit

After images work in color as well as black and white. Look at this bowl of fruit. Nobody wants to eat a blue banana or a turquoise apple, but you can make the fruit look the way it should.

Take a piece of plain white paper, and put it beside the book. Hold the book under a bright light and stare at the purple apple in the middle of the picture on the opposite page. Keep looking straight at it for at least one minute without blinking, and then look at the white paper. Now remember to keep blinking and you will see a perfectly ordinary bowl of fruit.

Your eye has reversed the colors. Just as black and white are opposites, or a complementary pair, so all the colors have their opposites—for example, blue and yellow, green and purple, and red and turquoise. If you stare at one color, the eye's special receptors for that particular color gradually become tired, so that when you look at the white sheet of paper, they are less active than the other receptors and you see the complementary color.

You can draw and color your own picture for an after image. Try using different shades to produce after images in a range of colors.

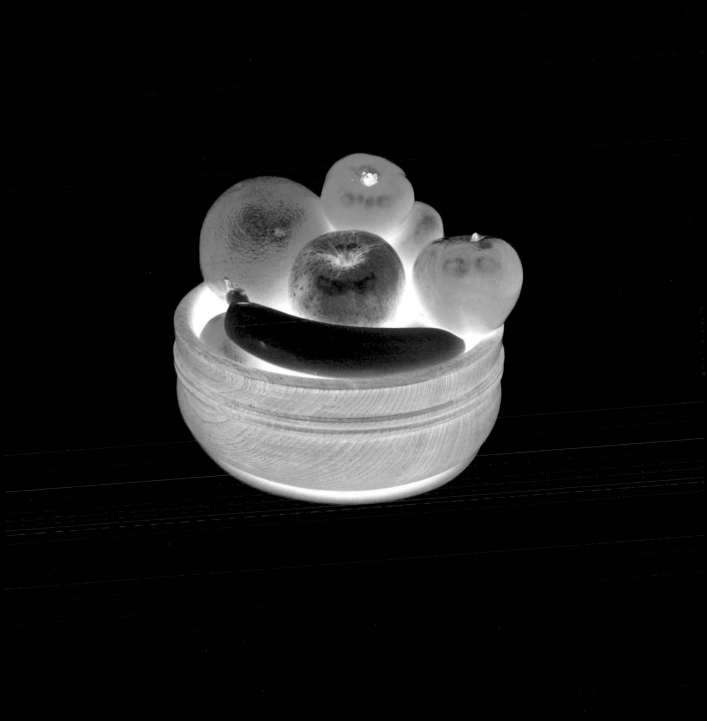

Impossible Shapes

Try counting the planks. Do you see three, or four? Now look at the fork. How many prongs does it have? Take a look at the shelves. There is apparently one ball on the top shelf, but how many on the bottom shelf? Or is it the middle shelf?

These strange shapes can exist only on paper. A clever illusion has been created with lines and angles carefully drawn to trick the eye and confuse the brain.

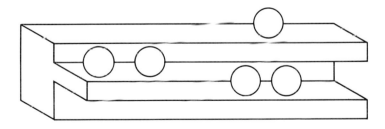

Stretched Shape, Secret Message

To make sense of this elongated shape, place the bottom edge of the book beneath your chin and tilt the top of the book slightly downward. You will then see the long, thin shape in the correct perspective and also be able to read the message.

Moving Picture

Hold the book up at arm's length and look at this picture of a parrot and its cage. Still looking at the picture, bring the book closer and closer to your eyes. If you bring the book close enough, the parrot will appear to be in its cage.

Magic Dots

These red and green dots are hiding something. To find out what it is, put on your 3-D glasses found at the back of the book, and look again. If you don't see the shape immediately, just keep looking, and watch it slowly appear.

The pattern here has been designed to trick the brain into seeing three-dimensionally. Your eyeballs are about two and a half inches apart, so each eye sees a different view. To test this, hold up one finger about six inches from the end of your nose. Look at your finger, quickly closing one eye at a time. Although you are holding your finger very still, it will appear to jump from side to side. This is because each eye has a slightly different view of it.

When both eyes work together, your brain uses the two different pictures to give you three-dimensional vision. When you look at the pattern of dots without the glasses, they all are the same distance away, and the picture looks flat. But when you put the glasses on, each eye views a different image, depending on which color it is looking through.

Once you have seen the hidden shape, reverse the glasses, and you will see the shape once more—but with an important difference. What is it? Turn to page 56 for the answer. For an additional 3-D effect, lean backward and forward, and from side to side while looking through the glasses.

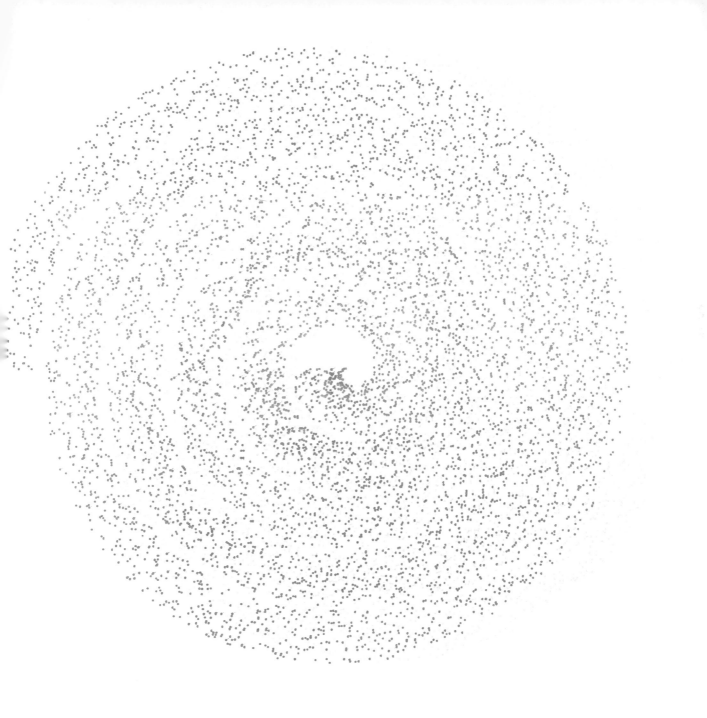

Straight Lines and Circles

old the book at arm's length and look at the shapes outlined in red. They look a little squashed. Now move the book slowly closer to your eyes. The shapes will alter until they become a perfect circle and square.

The background of radiating lines makes these shapes appear distorted at first. When you bring the picture closer, your eyes are forced to focus on the shapes instead of the lines.

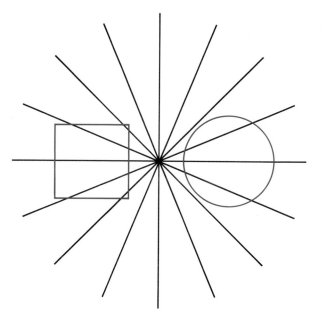

Which of these two red circles is bigger?

The circle in the center on the right looks much smaller than the one on the left. But if you measure them, you'll find that they are exactly the same size.

We naturally compare the red circles with the circles that surround them. The large circles make the red circle on the right appear smaller, and the smaller ones make the red circle on the left look larger.

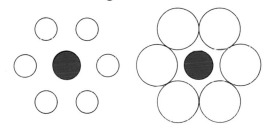

Are these red lines straight or curved?

By taking a ruler and placing it along the lines, you will see that they are both straight.

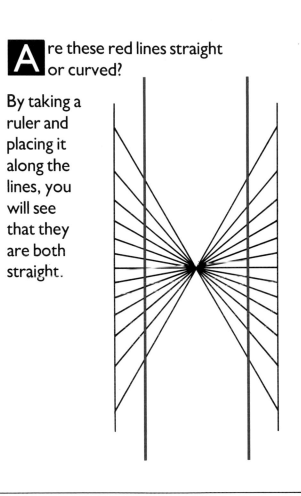

More Magic Dots

This is another pattern like the one on page 21. Put on your 3-D glasses (green "glass" over left eye, red "glass" over right eye) and look at the picture. Keep looking at it, and something will come out of the dots toward you. Now reverse the glasses, and it will recede back into the page. The effect is even stronger if you place a coin or small object at the center of the picture while you're looking through the glasses. Or watch your hand enter a "tunnel" as you point to the center of the shape.

The Vegetable Gardener

T his picture looks perfectly normal: a dark green bowl, filled with different vegetables and nuts. But the title of the picture is "The Vegetable Gardener," not "The Bowl of Vegetables." Turn the book upside down and you will see why.

Giuseppe Arcimboldo, who painted this picture, was a sixteenth-century Italian artist. His speciality was bizarre paintings of faces composed entirely of vegetables, fruits, flowers, and sometimes even animals and birds.

The Third Dimension

All pictures are two-dimensional. They have height and width. The third dimension, depth, is missing. To give this picture a third dimension, put on your 3-D glasses with the green "glass" over the left eye and the red "glass" over the right.

The red part of the image represents the view from one eye, and the green part represents the view from the other. The glasses allow one eye to see the red image and the other eye to see the green image, so that when you look with both eyes, you no longer see a double image, but a single one in three dimensions.

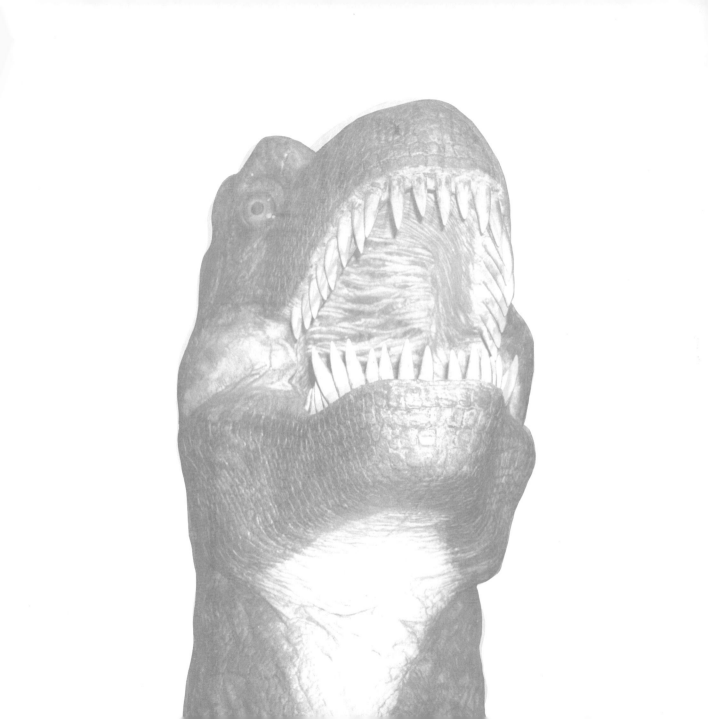

Something Fishy

This is another of Arcimboldo's extraordinary paintings. The man's head, in profile, is made up of different kinds of fish and sea creatures. If you look closely, you can pick out a seal, a crab, an octopus, a shark, and a turtle. If you find it difficult to see the man's face, you can follow the clues at the bottom of the page.

Once you have managed to trace the man's profile, your brain will adjust to the fact that this picture can be seen in two ways.

(The shark's mouth is the man's mouth, the head of a fish is his nose, and a mussel is his ear. The ray is his cheek.)

More of the Third Dimension

Here is another picture that needs an extra dimension, like the one on page 29. Take a look at it through your 3-D glasses with the green "glass" over the left eye and the red "glass" over the right.

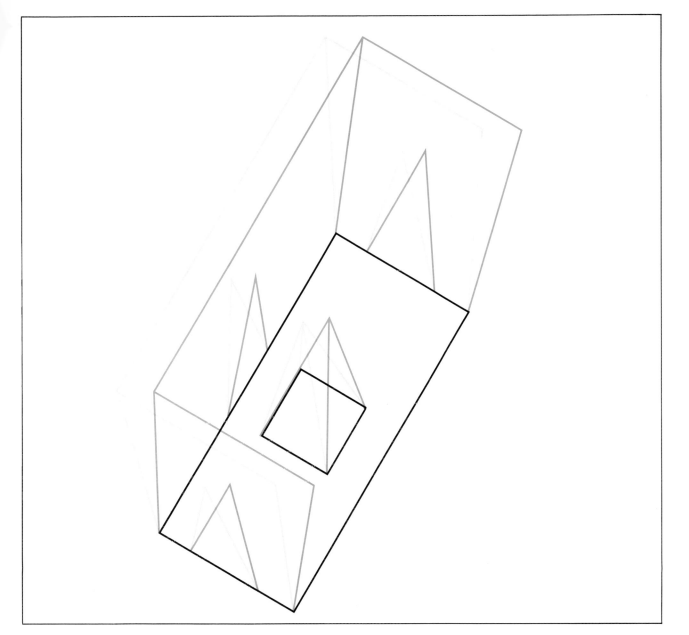

Op Art

Op artists use complex patterns to make the viewer experience movement when looking at their pictures. The lines and shapes actually seem to move up and down on the page. Look at this picture—no matter how long you look or how hard you try, you cannot make it keep still.

When you look at anything, your brain receives information about it from your eyes. It is your brain that tells you, "It is a dog" or "It is a house." When you look at Op Art, your brain does its best to try and make sense of the patterns, but keeps coming to different conclusions about them. It keeps shifting from one answer to another, which makes the patterns appear to move.

The Hidden Face

Hold the pattern on the opposite page about two inches away from your nose and look at it carefully. Now slowly move the book further and further away, and you will discover a hidden picture. The more distance there is between your eyes and the picture, the clearer it will become.

This Is Not a Spiral

Everything about this picture convinces us that we are looking at a spiral. In fact, this is a series of circles with lines drawn through them, carefully shaded to give the illusion of a spiral.

To prove that these are circles, trace one or more with your finger, starting on the outside—but be warned, it will be much harder than it sounds. Near the center of the picture the illusion of the spiral is so strong, it can influence your finger's movement.

Double Portraits

This face looks quite happy— but try turning it upside down and see what happens!

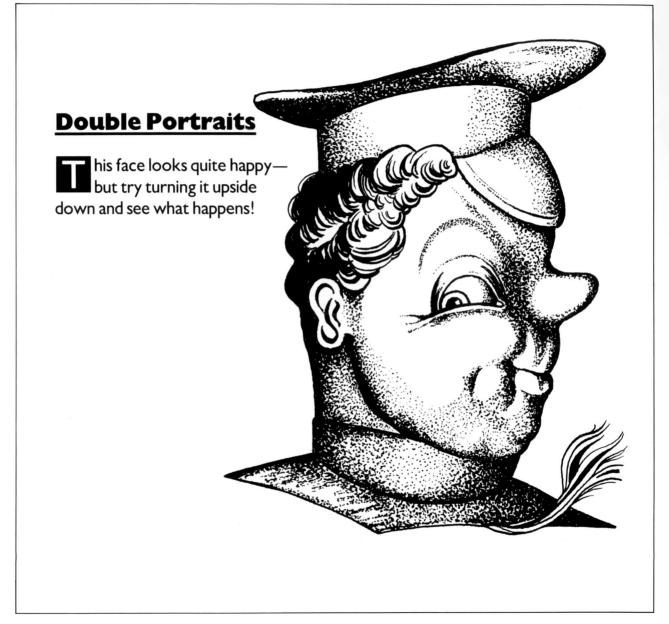

What do you see here: a young girl, or an old woman? Or both?

(Clues: The girl's ear is one of the old woman's eyes. Her neck band is the old woman's mouth.)

Two Pictures in One

Look at the drawing in the left hand corner below. It is obviously a fish, but the drawings that follow it have been carefully altered so that gradually you see something else. What is it?

The fish changes into a king's head. The drawings on the left appear more readily to be a fish, and those on the right to be a king's head. The fifth one in the sequence appears as either, depending on how you look at it.

Take a look at the picture on the right. What is it?

This is either a picture of a vase, or of two faces in profile. It can be interpreted in two different ways, depending on whether you see the black outline or the white outline.

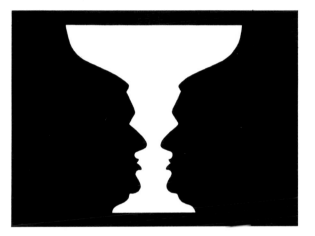

Disappearing Dots

Look at this grid pattern. You will notice that there seems to be a gray dot at the center of each white cross. If you stare at each cross individually, you will see that particular dot vanish.

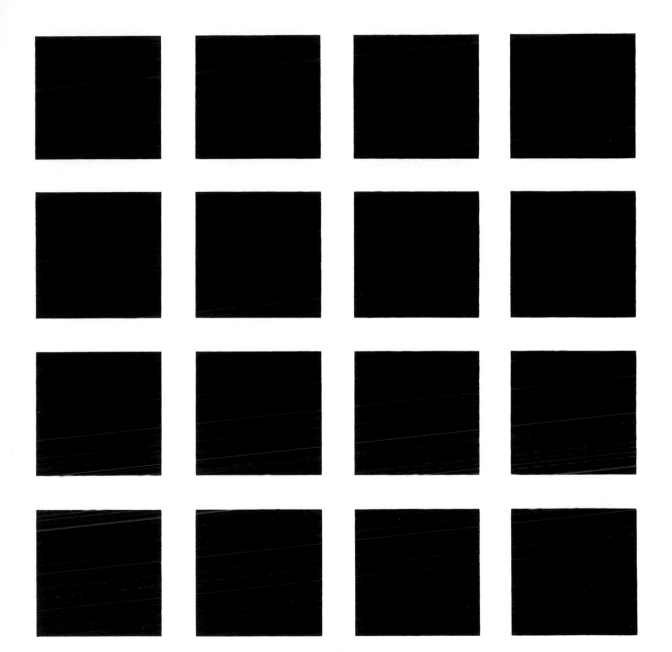

The Pendulum Experiment

This is an experiment for two people. You will need a piece of string with something fairly heavy, such as a bunch of keys, tied to the end of it to make a pendulum. The string should be about three feet long. You will also need your 3-D glasses.

Ask your friend to stand on a chair and swing the pendulum from side to side in a straight line. Watch the pendulum swinging for a few seconds. Now take the glasses. Look through the red "glass" with one eye, leaving the other eye uncovered and open.

Watch the pendulum swinging once more. What happens to it?

The pendulum is no longer swinging in a straight line. It is going around in a circle. If you switch the red "glass" of the glasses to your other eye, the pendulum will appear to trace a circle in the opposite direction. Keep looking through the red "glass" and ask your friend to place an object just behind the swinging pendulum. When you watch the pendulum swinging now, it will appear to go through the object each time it swings around.

Two-way Shapes

When you look at this shape, one of the sections appears to be solid, and the other to be just an empty space. Look again—the sections are the other way around. The left and right sections seem to take turns coming "forward." After a while you are able to make the sections flip-flop in and out at will.

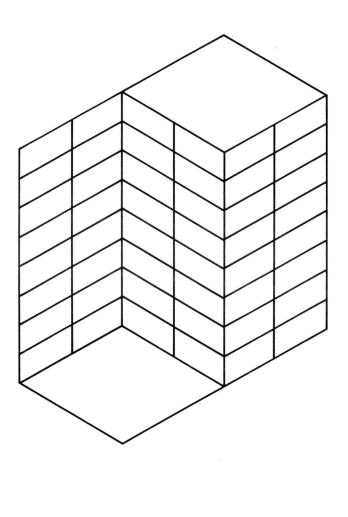

Look at the rectangle below. Can you make
it stay still? The lines have been drawn in such
a way that its shape keeps altering.

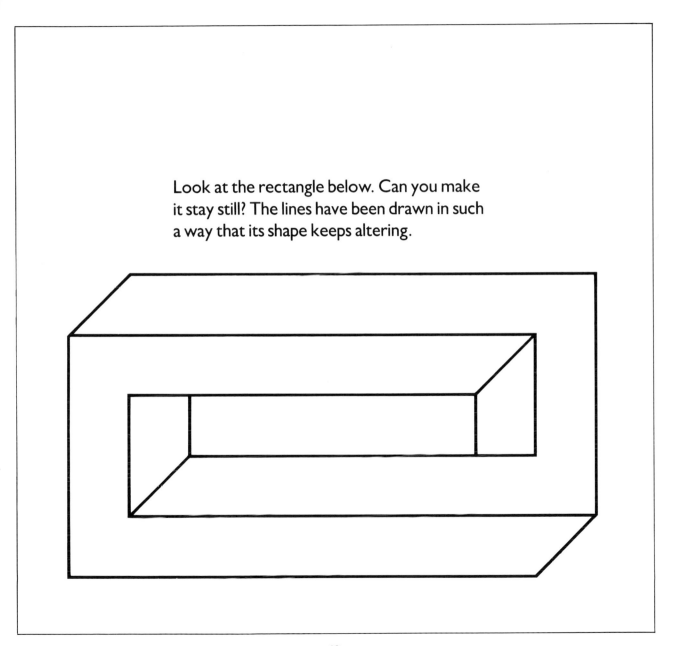

Look Inside Your Own Eye

All you need to see the inside of your own eye is a small light—and a friend to help. Make sure that the room is completely dark, and then have your friend shine the light into your pupil from below, or onto the white of your eye. The light should be moved gently from side to side. After about thirty seconds, you will begin to see an orange background with black lines that look like the branches of a tree. You are now looking at the back of your own eye.

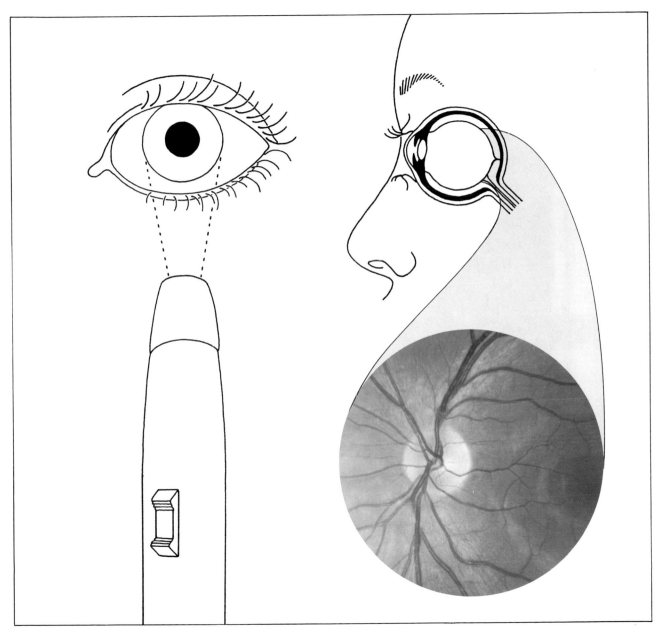

Upstairs, Downstairs

At first glance this picture looks like an ordinary house. But study the staircase at the top of the house. What is wrong with it? Try to find the top and bottom steps. Now try tracing it with your finger, starting at what you think is the bottom step. The staircase appears to be going up—and yet the "top" step and the "bottom" step are next to each other.

This drawing is the work of a Dutch artist named M. C. Escher. He purposely combined different perspectives in order to confuse the eyes of the viewer.

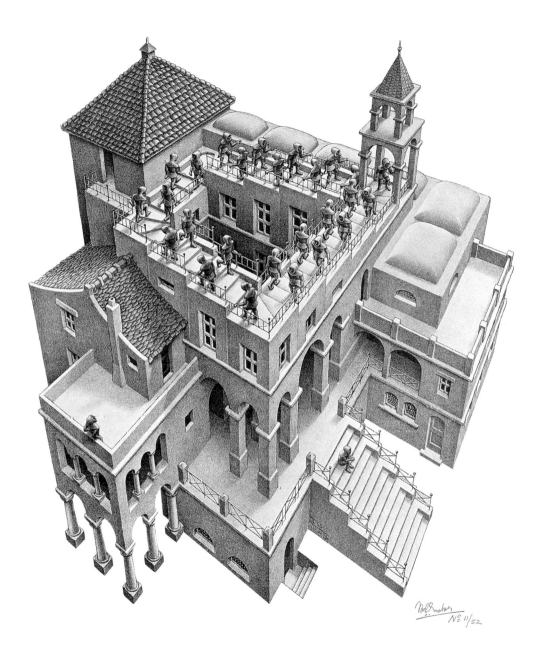

53

Color the Clown

This clown looks dull in his black and white suit. Let's give him some color.

First make sure that the book is held at a fixed distance from your eye. Look at the red stripes on the facing page while you count slowly up to ten. Now look at the green stripes and count slowly to ten again. Repeat this at least twenty times. It should take about five minutes. It might be easier to have a friend keep track of the time while you count.

Look back at the clown, keeping the book in the same position. His suit will now be green and red. If you turn the book sideways, you'll see the colors have switched.

Although it will only take five minutes to get this effect, if you look at the red and green stripes for a longer time—say, ten or fifteen minutes—before looking at the clown, the effect should last for longer. Try looking at the clown again the following day, and you may find that he's still wearing his red and green suit.

Magic Colors

Press out the disk at the back of the book, and place it firmly on the tip of a pencil. Spin the pencil around between the palms of your hands, and watch closely. . . . What has happened?

If the disk is spun clockwise, you will see three rings of color appear—blue on the outside, green in the middle, and red on the inside. If it is spun in the opposite direction, the colors will appear in reverse order— red on the outside, green in the middle, and blue on the inside. The spinning of the pattern on the disk tricks the eyes and brain into seeing color.

Answers

p. 8 Clown face

p. 9 Marilyn Monroe

p. 21 The spiral appears either to emerge out of the page toward you, or to retreat into the page away from you, depending on which way you are wearing the glasses.

p. 13 The Mona Lisa by Leonardo da Vinci

Visual Magic Is All Around Us

Now that you have seen the visual magic in this book, why not look for illusions around you? You can look for visual magic wherever you are. For example, if you see a waterfall, try staring at it for a few minutes. Then look at the trees and rocks beside the waterfall. They will probably appear to be moving upward—but of course they are still fixed to the ground! Or have you ever noticed that the moon looks larger when it is close to the horizon than when it is high in the sky? In fact the size of the moon never changes—it is a visual illusion.

Try watching the wheels of a train or car traveling at high speed. The wheels do not appear to be moving at all, but they are really just spinning around too fast for us to see the movement. Illusions may also occur because we see what we expect to see, rather than what is really there. If you read the sentence, "The quick brown fox jumps over the the lazy dog," you may miss the fact that "the" appears twice before "lazy dog."

Our brains work incredibly fast, and can jump to the wrong conclusion. But most of the time our eyes and brain are very good at telling us about the world around us. Whatever fun we have with illusions, it will be a long time before we can manufacture anything that is as sensitive, fast, and adaptable as the human visual system.

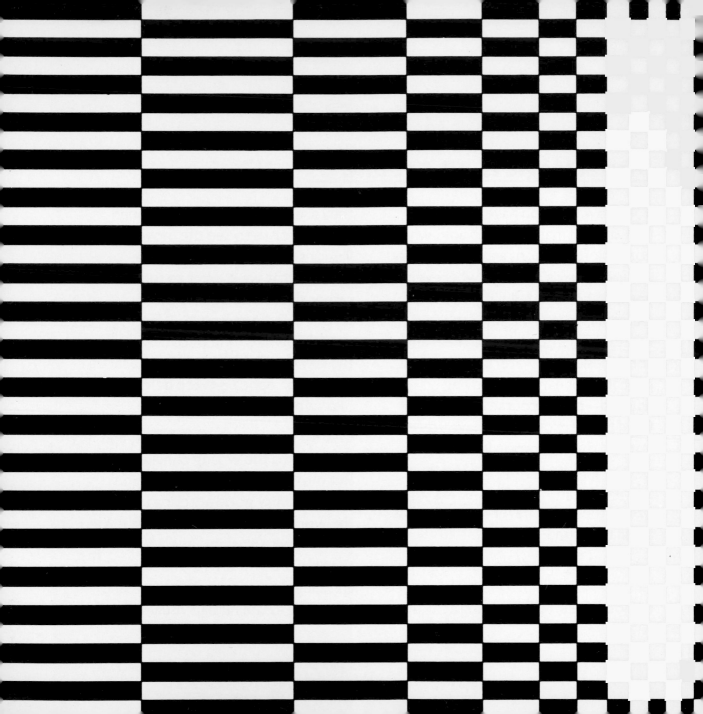

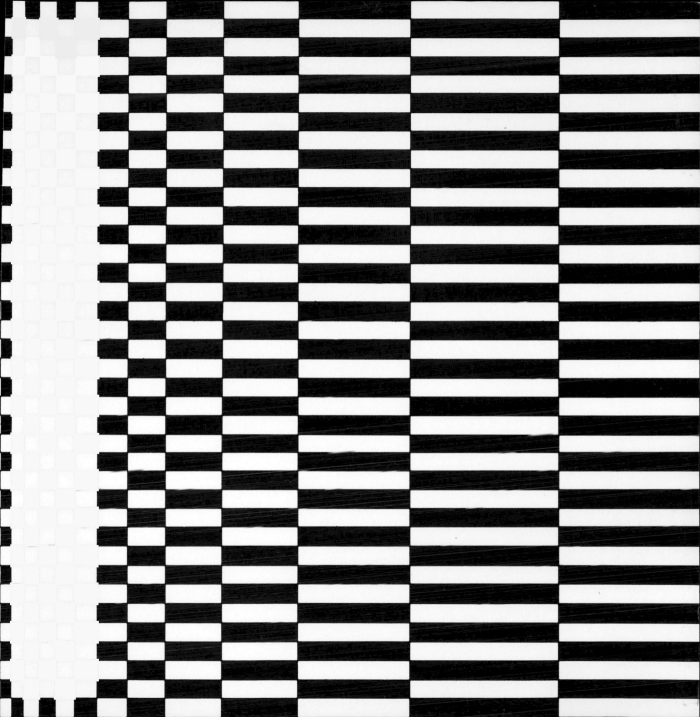